She
Persisted

....

PATSY MINK

....

— INSPIRED BY —

She Persisted

by Chelsea Clinton & Alexandra Boiger

....

PATSY MINK

....

Written by
Tae Keller

Interior illustrations by
Gillian Flint

PHILOMEL

⎰ For all the kids ⎱
marching ahead of the majority

PHILOMEL BOOKS
An imprint of Penguin Random House LLC, New York

First published in the United States of America by Philomel Books,
an imprint of Penguin Random House LLC, 2022

Text copyright © 2022 by Chelsea Clinton
Illustrations copyright © 2022 by Alexandra Boiger

Visit us online at penguinrandomhouse.com.

Library of Congress Cataloging-in-Publication Data is available.

Printed in the United States of America

HC ISBN 9780593402887
10 9 8 7 6 5 4 3 2 1
PB ISBN 9780593402900
10 9 8 7 6 5 4 3 2 1

WOR

Edited by Jill Santopolo and Talia Benamy.
Design by Ellice M. Lee.
Text set in LTC Kennerley.

DEAR READER,

As Sally Ride and Marian Wright Edelman both powerfully said, "You can't be what you can't see." When Sally said that, she meant that it was hard to dream of being an astronaut, like she was, or a doctor or an athlete or anything at all if you didn't see someone like you who already had lived that dream. She especially was talking about seeing women in jobs that historically were held by men.

I wrote the first *She Persisted* and the books that came after it because I wanted young girls—and children of all genders—to see women who worked hard to live their dreams. And I wanted all of us to see examples of persistence in the face of different challenges to help inspire us in our own lives.

I'm so thrilled now to partner with a sisterhood of writers to bring longer, more in-depth versions of these stories of women's persistence and achievement to readers. I hope you enjoy these chapter books as much as I do and find them inspiring and empowering.

And remember: If anyone ever tells you no, if anyone ever says your voice isn't important or your dreams are too big, remember these women. They persisted and so should you.

Warmly,
Chelsea Clinton

She
Persisted

....

She Persisted: WANGARI MAATHAI

She Persisted: WILMA MANKILLER

She Persisted: PATSY MINK

She Persisted: SALLY RIDE

She Persisted: MARGARET CHASE SMITH

She Persisted: SONIA SOTOMAYOR

She Persisted: MARIA TALLCHIEF

She Persisted: DIANA TAURASI

She Persisted: HARRIET TUBMAN

She Persisted: OPRAH WINFREY

She Persisted: MALALA YOUSAFZAI

PATSY MINK

TABLE OF CONTENTS

....

······························

A Sunny Childhood

Patsy Matsu Takemoto was born in 1927 on the island of Maui, in Hawaii. Maui was a land of sunshine, white sand beaches, and warm trade winds. But though the island was beautiful, its people were going through a difficult time.

In 1898, the United States annexed Hawaii. This meant that the US government stole control of the islands from the Hawaiian people and declared Hawaii a US "territory." This was a dark time for many Native Hawaiians, who lost their homeland to incoming mainland Americans.

Additionally, because Hawaii was just a territory and not yet a state, the US offered Hawaii's citizens very few protections or rights, and the people of Hawaii had little control over governing their own lives or what was happening in their communities.

At the time, the US government saw the islands as a place they could use for their own benefit, without thinking about the people who lived there. The government set up a military base on Oahu called Pearl Harbor and, through taxes, made money off the islands' businesses—especially the booming business of growing sugar.

Like many people of Japanese descent in Hawaii, Patsy grew up on a sugar plantation.

For most plantation workers—mostly Native Hawaiians at first, and later, in Patsy's time, Asian immigrants—this was a difficult life of endless, grueling work in the fields.

But Patsy's childhood was different. She was lucky. Many of the other kids her age had parents who'd just arrived in Hawaii from Japan, but Patsy's parents had grown up in Hawaii. Because of this, Patsy's dad spoke English natively, so he was hired as a civil engineer for the plantation, instead of a field worker. This led to more money and less back-breaking labor for his family.

Patsy grew up in a comfortable cottage surrounded by palm trees, sugarcane, and dirt roads. Some days, she would play with the pigs, chickens, rabbits, and turkeys. Other days, she would spend time at the nearby beach, searching for seashells.

On the very best days, she would play with her brother, Eugene. Just a year older, he was Patsy's best friend, and together they would run, explore, and venture into the nearby mountains to pick mushrooms or bamboo.

Although Patsy grew up in a time when girls were often expected to stay home while boys played outside, her family always treated her and her brother as equals. Eugene included her in football and baseball games, and her parents encouraged her to follow her dreams.

And Patsy was certainly a dreamer. It didn't take long before she found her first dream. When she was four, she woke up to a sharp pain in her stomach, and when her parents rushed her to the hospital, the family doctor realized she needed emergency surgery to remove her appendix. That must have been scary for four-year-old Patsy! But her doctor comforted her, and the surgery helped Patsy feel better.

From that point on, she looked up to her family physician. He had saved her, and perhaps even better, he had shown her that saving other people was *possible*. Though she'd never seen a female doctor, she knew she wanted to be one. She wanted to comfort, care for, and heal others.

She was lucky to have a family who let her dream, but when Patsy reached fourth grade, the prejudices of the outside world began to press in on her happy childhood. Patsy and Eugene had been doing so well in school that their parents decided to move them to a well-regarded school called Kaunoa English Standard School. The students there needed to pass an English grammar test in order to go to the school, so most Native Hawaiian and Asian kids— who often spoke English as a second language and didn't have formal training—were rejected.

Because of this, 95 percent of the students at Patsy's new school were white. The teachers were all white. And Patsy felt like an outsider. Very few of her classmates lived on a plantation like she did, and she didn't make many friends. Despite her excellent grades, her teachers didn't pay much attention to her.

But Patsy continued to work hard, getting good grades so she could eventually become a

doctor. She explored other interests, too. After school, she would listen to President Franklin Delano Roosevelt speaking on the radio, and felt inspired by his big plans.

When she wasn't listening to the radio, she would sit in a mango tree, surrounded by the sweet scent of ripe fruit, and read Mahatma Gandhi's writings aloud. Gandhi was a civil rights leader in India, whose activism inspired people throughout the world. Like many others, Patsy was drawn to his ideas about nonviolence and peaceful protest to expand rights and opportunities for all people.

Some evenings, her dad even took her to election rallies. Together, they'd sit Hawaiian style on the grass, listening to Hawaiian music and watching politicians give speeches about democracy. Though she was still focused on medicine, it's easy to see how these experiences planted the seeds for her future in politics.

"Politics was an important thing," she said later in life, when she reflected on those early election rallies. "Being a citizen was important."

Patsy's childhood was not perfect, but it was a good one—until tenth grade. On December 7th, 1941, just one day after her fourteenth birthday, bombs fell on Hawaii, and they changed everything.

CHAPTER 2

Trouble

In 1941, Japan dropped bombs on Pearl Harbor, the major US military base in Hawaii.

Japan was on the side of the Axis Powers during World War II, along with Germany, and the United States hadn't yet joined the fight against them. But when Japan attacked Hawaii—a terrible shock at 7:45 in the morning—over 2,000 Americans died. From that point on, the United States officially entered World War II, fighting both Germany and Japan.

This was scary enough already, especially living in Hawaii, where the attack was so close to home. But in addition to going to war with foreign countries, the US government also turned on its own citizens. Japanese American citizens, who had lived in America their whole lives, were suddenly treated like the enemy, just for being ethnically Japanese.

Over 120,000 Japanese Americans were taken from their homes and imprisoned in concentration camps across the country. Many of these camps were kept in horrible condition, without kitchens or even working toilets. People were packed into tiny spaces, without any privacy, and the camps were surrounded by barbed wire and armed guards.

These camps were morally wrong and should have been illegal. Sending people there denied them their fundamental human rights, like freedom and dignity. But that didn't stop the US government.

It was a terrifying time to be Japanese in the United States, and Patsy watched in helpless horror as her own government locked her friends and teachers away in these camps. Nobody knew if they would be next.

One evening, Patsy's greatest fear came true. Her father was arrested and taken away for questioning. It was a terrible, sleepless night not knowing if she would ever see him again. Thankfully, the government decided not to send him away. He returned to his family the next day, but the fear never left. As Patsy watched him burn all his precious Japanese items the next morning—family heirlooms from Patsy's grandparents that he feared would make him seem more

connected to Japan than to the US—she knew she would never forget this.

"It made me realize that [I] could not take citizenship and the promise of the US Constitution for granted," she later said.

Unfortunately, discrimination, or unfair treatment, based on their Japanese heritage didn't just come from the government. The cruelty toward

Japanese Americans seeped into all aspects of Patsy's life. She'd become used to unfriendliness from some of her white classmates, but it was much worse now. They taunted her and called her mean names.

And yet, despite all this, Patsy never forgot her dream. She worked hard, and two years later, during her senior year of high school, she ran for class president. She won—and became the first girl ever elected in her school.

With the highest grades in her class and a record as class president, she went on to college at the University of Hawaii, where she joined the debate team and quickly became elected president of the premed club—a club for students who wanted to be doctors.

She was enjoying her time at the university,

but by her sophomore year, she noticed that many of her friends were moving from Hawaii to colleges on the mainland, seeking bigger and better opportunities. Following suit, Patsy transferred to Wilson College, a small college in Pennsylvania.

But Wilson College was not what she expected. As soon as she arrived, the president brought her into his office and told her that since English was not her first language, she would have difficulty making friends and succeeding in class. He had assumed that because she was Japanese, she could not speak English. He did not understand that she could be both Japanese *and* American.

Wilson College was not a good environment for her, so Patsy moved to the University of Nebraska. But there she found more challenges. The college housing was segregated, which meant that Asian, Black, and Latinx students were not allowed to live on campus with the white students. Patsy was horrified by this injustice, and she decided to do something about it.

She wrote letters to the university, the campus newspaper, and the local newspapers to explain

that this was not okay, and she encouraged other students to write letters as well. She gave speeches on the issue. She talked to anybody who would listen. She became, in her words, "somebody who was going to stir up trouble."

Other students began to follow her lead. Inspired, they formed a group and elected her president. And the speeches and letter writing *worked*.

The next year, the school changed its housing policy. Patsy was victorious! And now she was determined to do even more.

CHAPTER 3

Forging Her Path

After making such a positive change in college, Patsy was ready to fulfill her childhood dream. She applied to over a dozen medical schools, but soon enough, the rejections began to roll in.

Letter after letter said the same thing: the schools did not want to accept a woman.

Patsy was heartbroken. "It was the most devastating disappointment of my life," she said.

Forced to find a new dream, Patsy applied to

law school, and was accepted into the University of Chicago Law School—where she was one of only two women in her graduating class. The classes there were competitive, and many of the students wanted the world to stay exactly as it was. Not everyone wanted to fight for change and equality like Patsy did.

But still, she was able to find a good group of friends. She studied hard and played cards in the campus lounge to relax. Occasionally, a man named John Mink played cards with her. In John's eyes, Patsy and her friends were like "a galaxy of very bright personalities"—and Patsy was at the center.

Though she secretly thought John was terrible at cards, Patsy was drawn to him. The two talked about science and books, about big ideas and bigger dreams. They shared the same beliefs about change and equality. And before long, they fell in love.

Not everyone understood their love, though. John was white, and some people didn't think a white person and an Asian person should be together. In some states, even in 1951, marriage between people of different races was still illegal.

Even worse, Patsy's own parents didn't approve of the relationship. Part of this was because they wanted Patsy to focus on her studies—but part of it was because they didn't want Patsy to be with a white man. They had lived through so much racism and discrimination, and they might have worried that John would be like so many of the white people they'd interacted with. They wanted Patsy to be with someone who would treat her like an equal.

But Patsy trusted John, and she trusted herself to make the right decision. Six months after meeting, they married. A few months later, they graduated. John found a job quickly, but nobody wanted to hire a female lawyer, and Patsy struggled.

The following year, during a blisteringly hot Chicago summer, Patsy gave birth to their baby girl, Gwendolyn, and the young family moved back to Hawaii—this time to the island of Oahu, home to the capital city, Honolulu.

Patsy had always loved Hawaii. The islands were part of her, and she was excited to return, eager to raise her newborn baby in the place she'd always called home.

But her home was not so kind when she returned.

When she began looking for a job as a lawyer, she got the same result as with medical school: rejection after rejection after rejection. Law firms didn't want to hire a woman. They told her that mothers shouldn't be working with, and that she needed to spend her time at home, taking care of her husband and baby.

They looked at her, a young mother, and

assumed her only priority should be her home. They didn't care that Patsy's parents also looked after her daughter, who everyone called Wendy. They didn't care that Wendy had a happy, loving childhood. They just looked at Patsy and assumed.

But if anyone thought she would give up based on the opinions of people who didn't know what they were talking about, they didn't know Patsy. Determined to do the job she'd trained so hard for, Patsy decided that if none of the companies would hire her, she would start her own. She rented an office in downtown Honolulu and filled it with borrowed furniture. With that, she became the first Asian American woman to practice law in Hawaii. It had been a difficult road to find work—and get paid for that work—but Patsy had been determined.

One night, a friend invited her to a meeting about the Democratic Party in Honolulu, and Patsy found herself in the world of politics. Maybe that meeting brought back memories of warm evenings watching speeches with her dad, and peaceful afternoons reading Gandhi in the mango trees. Maybe she also realized that her childhood dream wasn't just about becoming a doctor—it was also about *helping* people. And politics was a way to help.

Patsy saw that the Democratic Party needed more young people, and she got involved immediately. The Republican Party in Hawaii was filled with older white businessmen, but she knew the Democratic Party there could be younger and more diverse—the party of the people. She started the Young Democrats club, which led, in part, to a revolution in Hawaiian politics. Politics no longer belonged to the wealthy older white people. It was for young people of all races—people who wanted change.

In 1956, a seat opened in the territorial House of Representatives. While Hawaii wasn't yet a US state and didn't have anyone representing them in Congress, they did have local elected officials. In the US, each state has its own government that works to create laws and systems that help the people in that state. Since Hawaii was still a territory, the group that did that work for them was called the territorial House of Representatives, and its members could speak up for Hawaii's citizens and make changes in its local government.

Patsy had found a new dream: she wanted to be one of those people. She wanted that job.

Of course, there were challenges when Patsy decided to run for office. Though the newspapers mentioned her qualifications as a lawyer and president of the Young Democrats, they also focused on her abilities as a housewife. Interviewers asked her if she did the housework at home, and one wrote that she was "just another housewife and mother when business hours [were] over."

None of the newspapers focused on the home lives of the men running.

Another problem was that she didn't fit in with the rest of the Democrat politicians. Though they were friendly to her face, her gender made her an outsider, and they made comments to make her feel small. They didn't take her seriously, and referred to her as "their little bowlegged Japanese doll."

On top of all this, Patsy didn't have as much money to spend on her campaign as her opponents did. But she wasn't going to let any of that stop her. If voters didn't take her seriously, she would *show* them her intelligence and determination. While her opponents spent money on big parties and festivals with balloons and musical performances, Patsy walked door to door to introduce herself to voters and talk about her beliefs.

To the surprise of many male Democrats, Patsy won the election and became the only woman in Hawaii's territorial congress.

Patsy Mink was a rising star.

CHAPTER 4

Fighting for Equality

When Patsy entered Hawaii's territorial government, she had one main goal: she wanted to make sure that everyone had equal rights.

One way she did that was to try to pass a bill (the first step to creating a law) that would make sure men and women in Hawaii received equal pay for doing equal work. Fighting for equality was not always easy, though, and she faced discrimination from many of the men she worked with. In a meeting with the other territorial senators, one of her male coworkers said, while Patsy sat right beside him, "We'll leave the woman out of it. This is a man's world."

The newspapers and radio stations didn't treat her much better. One radio station criticized her almost daily because she fought to stop the US from creating and testing nuclear bombs. Though many of the other territorial senators, including her friend Dan Inouye, said the same things as Patsy, the radio always focused on Patsy, calling her names and saying she couldn't be trusted.

It was hard to avoid these comments, and Patsy's daughter, Wendy, who was six at the time, often overheard them. When Wendy asked her mom about it, Patsy explained that sometimes people have extreme reactions to things they don't

agree with. But, Patsy told her daughter, other people's reactions never made her want to step down or be quiet. She also turned the attacks into a teachable moment, reminding her daughter that no matter how much they disagreed with someone, it was wrong to call anyone mean names.

In 1957, after years of fighting and not giving up, Patsy's equal pay for equal work bill finally passed. This was a huge victory, not only for Patsy, but for women throughout Hawaii. Patsy knew from experience how hard it was to get a job as a woman—and she knew how hard it was to get *paid* for that job. This bill was important to her because it meant other women didn't have to struggle quite as hard as she had.

In 1959, just a couple years after her bill passed, the US government announced that Hawaii was changing from a territory to an official state. Many Democrats considered this a big victory, because now Hawaii received equal treatment from the US government as every other state. Hawaii's official statehood status also came with new positions in the US government. Now Hawaii could send two senators and one congressperson to the national House of Representatives and Senate, where they could give Hawaii a voice in the country's politics.

Those positions were open, waiting to be filled.

And Patsy couldn't wait to fill one.

At first, it seemed that some of the popular men in the Democratic party, including Dan Inouye, would all run for senator, leaving the House seat open for Patsy. But the Democratic leaders pressured Dan to run against Patsy, and Patsy soon found herself in a heated election. She didn't expect her old friend to run against her, but she refused to give up. She knew she would do a good job in Congress.

But once Dan announced he was running, voters began to turn on Patsy. They said she was too young and too ambitious—criticisms that Dan, who was about the same age and had about the same amount of experience, did not receive.

Throughout the entire campaign, Patsy faced pressure from her opposition to step down and run for a lower position, which they said was "where she belonged." But she refused. Like she'd told Wendy, she would not let other people's reactions force her to be quiet.

She fought hard until the very end of the campaign, but this time, Patsy lost. That year, fewer than 4 percent of the national congresspeople were women. All of those women were white.

As one newspaper in Hawaii wrote, "People would rather send a man to Congress than a woman."

Patsy was devastated. She swore she'd never run again.

....

CHAPTER 5

Democracy and Determination

Losing the election hurt. Patsy was aware of the ways that being a woman, and specifically an Asian American woman, had hurt her chances. As strong as she was, living with that discrimination took its toll.

She knew people in America expected Asian American women to be quiet and unambitious, but that was an inaccurate and unfair stereotype. "It's extremely difficult," she said, "[for Asian women] to really make a stand on public issues without being labelled a radical or misfit."

With the weight of stereotypes and the pain of the loss, she was discouraged—but her despair didn't last long. She was fighting for equality, and the idea of helping others was bigger than her own struggles. A year after she lost the election for Congress, she was invited to Los Angeles to speak at the Democratic National Convention, a big gathering of all of the party's leaders.

If she felt nervous about giving a speech, nobody in the audience could tell. They only saw her strength and passion. Standing in front of the crowd, she declared, "If to believe in freedom and equality is to be a radical, then I am a radical!"

When another seat in Congress opened up in 1965, Patsy ran again. Hawaii had gotten a second seat in Congress based on the number of people who lived there, and Patsy wanted to represent them. As a symbol of her commitment, she got a Daruma doll. The traditional Japanese doll comes with both eyes undrawn. When someone starts a big project, they fill in one eye. When they finish, they fill in the other.

Before long, her Daruma doll had both eyes—because this time, Patsy won. She was going

to be a member of the US Congress, and the very first woman of color to be there.

Patsy Mink didn't waste any time in Congress before showing people what she believed in. On her first day on the job, she joined a few other members of Congress in protesting Mississippi's voting practices, which were unfair because they prevented Black citizens from voting.

Very few congresspeople participated in this protest, but being in the minority didn't bother Patsy. As she said: "It is easy enough to vote right and be consistently with the majority . . . but it is more often more important to be ahead of the majority and this means being willing to . . . stand alone for a while if necessary."

Throughout her time in Congress, Patsy always followed her moral compass and fought passionately for what she believed in. One of the issues that was always close to her heart was women's equality—and she often found herself fighting for that in her very own workplace.

For example, at work, there was a House gym, supposedly meant for all members of Congress. However, women were not allowed to use it. When Patsy asked the male congresspeople to reserve the gym for women for just a few hours a week, they refused.

"There are four hundred twenty-four of us," they said, "and only eleven of you."

But Patsy knew that wasn't fair. Women deserved to exercise, too. So when she saw a flyer inviting "members of Congress" to an exercise class in the gym, she spoke to some of the other female congresspeople and formed a plan.

When the class began, three of the women marched up to the gym. The guard stopped them, saying, "It's just for members of Congress." But of course, they *were* members of Congress.

Eventually, the guard explained that women weren't allowed, but Patsy and the other female congresspeople had made their point—and they made headlines, too. Newspapers all around the country reported on how they were "exercising their right to exercise."

Most newspapers said that the women were joking, but for Patsy, this was more than a joke. This was symbolic. "There are so many ways in which sex discrimination manifests itself," she explained. "You really have to make an issue whenever it strikes you to protest it . . . You can't tolerate it."

After all the attention, the male representatives finally allowed the women to use the gym for two hours every Tuesday and Thursday morning. It wasn't much, but it was something—something that wouldn't have happened without Patsy.

Patsy faced more instances of sexism, or worse treatment for women, in Congress, but she never, ever tolerated it. One instance came during a Democratic Party planning meeting. When Patsy asked if they had a plan for allowing women to one day become president, a doctor named Edgar Berman, one of the members of the committee, scoffed.

He told Patsy—and everyone else in that meeting—that women could not be leaders. That they were born incapable because their bodies were different.

Patsy knew how untrue and ridiculous that was, and it was even worse to hear it from a doctor—somebody who should have known better. It was dangerous for doctors to hold beliefs that were built on prejudice, rather than fact.

Furious, she turned to a strategy that had proven successful in the past: she wrote a letter. In it, she explained that Dr. Berman's sexism and false statements should not be tolerated.

Like the letter she'd written in college, this one convinced people, and Dr. Berman resigned from his position in the party leadership.

But Patsy didn't stop with fighting against the sexism in her workplace. She wanted to make life easier for all women around the country. Many of the bills she wrote and supported provided care to poor women and children, and improved the education system.

Education was something that mattered

deeply to Patsy. Her schooling and teachers had gotten her through some of the hardest years of her life. She also knew how hard it was for women to get into schools, because she'd been rejected from all those medical schools, and had been one of only *two* women in her graduating class in law school.

She was determined to give women the access she'd fought so hard for, and that determination led her to write Title IX, which many consider to be the most effective and important bill of her career.

With help from Representative Edith Green and Senator Birch Bayh, Patsy wrote this bill, which stated that no public school, from elementary all the way to college, could exclude girls and

women from activities and programs. Schools could no longer deny girls admission just because they were girls or women. And they couldn't deny girls scholarships or block them from sports teams. In fact, if schools invested in scholarships and sports for boys and men, they had to do the same for girls and women, too.

Title IX passed in the House and Senate and was signed by President Nixon with little pushback, and at first, it seemed like a simple victory. So many doors had been closed to Patsy, and now, for others, she'd opened them.

But soon enough, schools across the country began to realize what this meant. Many schools, especially the ones with big football teams, poured all their money into the men's sports. Title IX meant they had to spend a portion of that money on women's teams, to give women opportunities, too. Colleges didn't want to do that. They pushed back, arguing that they shouldn't have to consider women's equality in sports—that women didn't even want to play sports anyway.

In response, Republicans in the House and Senate attempted to rewrite Title IX so it wouldn't include sports. An important part of Title IX was that it told schools that girls and women must have access to athletics programs and school gyms. Now the Republican senators and congresspeople wanted to erase that.

This was all too familiar to Patsy. She'd exercised the right to exercise once before, right there in Congress. She knew it mattered. So she fought hard to keep Title IX intact. This led to a heated debate in Congress, with Patsy and some of her fellow Democrats passionately defending women's equality.

The vote was up in the air. Nobody knew which way it would go. But in the middle of this debate, Patsy received a devastating call. Her daughter, Wendy, had been in a terrible car accident, and the doctors didn't know if she'd survive the night.

Patsy left immediately, running from Congress with tears in her eyes.

Thankfully, Wendy survived and recovered, but the Republicans won by a single vote: Title IX would be rewritten. Because Patsy hadn't been there, she hadn't been able to vote. If she'd been there, it would have been a tie.

This would have been a huge loss for women's equality—but Representative Carl Bert Albert, a friend of Patsy's and an important member of Congress, explained to the other representatives why Patsy had to leave so suddenly. Many congresspeople felt deeply for her crisis, and they agreed to do a revote with Patsy there.

In the revote, Patsy's position won. Some Republicans even changed their vote after hearing her speak. Title IX was protected, and in the decades since the bill was passed, the number of women with college degrees has more than tripled, and girls and women have far more access to education and athletics. One example of its impact: In 1972, the year Title IX passed, about seven hundred girls played on high school soccer teams in the US. In 2019, 390,000 did.

With Title IX, Patsy Mink changed the lives of girls and women across the country.

....

CHAPTER 6

A Lasting Impact

In 1975, Patsy decided to run for a Senate seat that would be opening up the following year. She'd had some setbacks in the House of Representatives, but she'd had great successes as well, and she knew she could make an even bigger impact in the Senate.

But, as had become a constant in her life, Patsy faced the challenge of sexism. Six women were running for various Senate seats that year, but at the time, there were no women in the Senate, and Patsy was running against a male opponent in the Democratic primary.

Patsy worked hard on her campaign, but as the election results trickled in, the outcome became clear. All six women running that year had lost. She would not be in the Senate, and she could not return to her seat in Congress.

So instead, she returned home to Hawaii. There, she was elected to City Council, and she

worked hard for her community. Occasionally, Patsy missed working nationally, but she was happy to be in Hawaii politics again, the state she had always loved.

Fifteen years later, in 1990, when Patsy's old Congress seat opened up again, she hesitated. She wasn't sure she wanted to run again. Her defeat had been painful, and her time in Congress hadn't been easy. She'd faced discrimination. The media had sometimes been cruel.

But despite all that, she'd helped so many people. And she found the courage to run once again.

If she had a Daruma doll for this election, that one got two eyes as well, because she won. Patsy went back to Congress, excited and ready to push for change.

The 1990s, though, were a different time in politics. President Reagan had undone so many of the bills Patsy fought so hard to pass. Patsy found herself fighting, again, to protect equality.

But there were bright spots, too, and in those years, Patsy began to see the lasting effect of her work. When she was first elected, she'd been one of the few women in Congress, and the only woman of color. Now there were more—young women who'd looked at Patsy decades ago and seen that their dreams were possible.

Patsy dedicated her career to opening doors for women. She advocated for other women of color, for poor women, and for young girls. The bills she passed, like the equal pay for equal work bill, the Equal Opportunity in Education Act, and of course, Title IX, helped advance rights and opportunities for girls and women in the United States.

Patsy Mink persisted despite discrimination, and she spent her life fighting for equality. When she died in 2002, Congress renamed Title IX as the "Patsy T. Mink Equal Opportunity in Education Act." And in 2014, President Obama honored her with the Presidential Medal of Freedom, a medal given to people who have made great contributions to the country and the world.

Her legacy lives on, but her fight is not yet over. Like Patsy, you can persist in achieving your dreams and creating a better world for all.

HOW YOU CAN PERSIST

by *Tae Keller*

Many of the injustices Patsy Mink fought still exist today. But there are people around the country fighting for change. You can be one of them.

1. Patsy learned the importance of writing letters! Write a letter to your mayor, senators, or congresspeople about the issues you care about.

2. Run for student body government.

3. Today, the US still has multiple "territories," including Puerto Rico and Guam. Research them and learn more about their history.

4. Learn more about US history, including

the annexation of Hawaii and the Japanese American concentration camps during World War II. It's important to know the history of our country, because when we learn about previous mistakes, we can learn not to repeat them.

5. Stand up for others. If you see someone being treated unfairly, say something.

6. Dream big. Don't let anyone tell you you're not good enough to achieve your goals.

A note on terminology: During WWII, the US government referred to the detention centers for Japanese Americans as *concentration camps*, but in the years since, many people began calling them *internment camps* instead. However, *internment camp* does not reflect the terrible conditions and treatment that so many Japanese Americans endured. In 1998, the American Jewish Committee and the Japanese American National Museum wrote a joint statement agreeing that *concentration camp* is the appropriate and accurate term to use because "a concentration camp is a place where people were imprisoned not because of any crimes they have committed, but simply because of who they are . . . the people in power removed a minority group from the general population and the rest of society let it happen." We must be aware of our country's history in order to prevent these kinds of atrocities from happening again. The Supreme Court ruling that allowed these concentration camps wasn't overturned until 2018.

Acknowledgments

I grew up hearing about Patsy Mink's legacy but hadn't realized the full extent of her impact until this project. She was truly incredible, and I'm so grateful I got the opportunity to do this. A huge, huge thank-you to her family, especially Wendy Mink, who was kind enough to speak with me about her mother's life and send me an early copy of her new biography, *Fierce and Fearless: Patsy Takemoto Mink, First Woman of Color in Congress.*

Thank you also to Dawn Sinclair, Rachel Lau, and the Lau family for helping me research.

Thank you to Talia Benamy and Jill Santopolo for bringing me on to this project and guiding me in this process. I am also so appreciative of Shara Hardeson, Krista Ahlberg, Ellice Lee, the rest of the Philomel team, Penguin Random House, Greenhouse Literary Agency, and The Book Group.

And, of course, thank you to Chelsea Clinton, Alexandra Boiger, Gillian Flint, and the Persisterhood for bringing such a beautiful series into the world. I feel lucky to be a part of it.

ᘯ References ᘰ

Arinaga, Esther K., and Rene E. Ojiri. "Patsy Takemoto Mink." *Asian-Pacific Law & Policy Journal* vol. 4, no. 2 (2003): 575–576.

Bassford, Kimberlee. *Patsy Mink: Ahead of the Majority.* Honolulu: Making Waves Films, 2008.

Casey, Brian. "Inouye, Mink Meet in All-or-Nothing Battle." *The Honolulu Advertiser.* June 19, 1959.

Davidson, Sue. *A Heart in Politics: Jeannette Rankin and Patsy T. Mink.* Seattle: Seal Press, 1994.

"Gwendolyn Mink Oral History Interview." Office of the Historian, US House of Representatives. March 14, 2016. file:///C:/Users/uahlbkr/AppData/Local/Temp/mink-transcript.pdf.

Komai, Chris. "American Jewish Committee, Japanese

American National Museum Issue Joint Statement about Ellis Island Exhibit Set to Open April 3." Japanese American National Museum. janm.org/press /release/american-jewish-committee-japanese-american -national-museum-issue-joint-statement.

Matsuura, Patsy. "They Are Capable of Doing Many Things." *The Honolulu Advertiser.* November 17, 1958.

Mertens, Richard. "Legacy: Patsy Mink (1927–2002): A Tenacious and Determined Politician," *University of Chicago Magazine* vol. 105, no. 1 (October 2012): 46–49.

Mink, Gwendolyn. Interview with the author. July 12, 2021.

"Mink, Patsy Takemoto." US House of Representatives: History, Art & Archives. history.house.gov/People /detail/18329.

Okamura, Raymond. "The American Concentration Camps: A Cover-Up Through Euphemistic Terminology." *The Journal of Ethnic Studies* vol. 10, no. 3 (Fall 1982): 95–108. https://home.nps.gov /tule/learn/education/upload/ray_okamura.pdf.

"Politics, Personalities . . . Letters." *The Honolulu Advertiser.* June 24, 1959.

Silva, Noenoe K. *Aloha Betrayed: Native Hawaiian Resistance to American Colonialism.* Durham, NC: Duke University Press, 2007.

Slagle, Alton. "But He Tried So Hard!" *The Honolulu Advertiser.* March 11, 1959.

Takaki, Ronald. *Pau Hana: Plantation Life and Labor in Hawaii, 1835-1920.* Honolulu: University of Hawaii Press, 1984.

"Women Congressmen Insist on Exercising Their Right to Exercise." *Poughkeepsie Journal.* February 7, 1967.

"Women in America: Indicators of Social and Economic Well-Being." White House Council on Women and Girls (March 2011): 21. https://www2.census.gov /library/publications/2011/demo/womeninamerica.pdf.

Wu, Judy Tzu-Chun, and Gwendolyn Mink. *Fierce and Fearless: Patsy Takemoto Mink, First Woman of Color in Congress.* New York: New York University Press, 2022.

TAE KELLER is the Newbery Award–winning author of *When You Trap a Tiger* and *The Science of Breakable Things*. She grew up in Honolulu, Hawaii, where she subsisted on kimchi, purple rice, and stories. Now she writes about biracial girls trying to find their voices, and lives in Seattle with her husband and a multitude of books.

Photo credit: Saavedra Photography

You can visit Tae online at
taekeller.com
and follow her on Twitter
@taekeller
or on Instagram
@tae_keller

GILLIAN FLINT has worked as a professional illustrator since earning an animation and illustration degree in 2003. Her work has since been published in the UK, USA and Australia. In her spare time, Gillian enjoys reading, spending time with her family and puttering about in the garden on sunny days. She lives in the northwest of England.

Courtesy of the illustrator

You can visit Gillian Flint online at
gillianflint.com
or follow her on Twitter
@GillianFlint
and on Instagram
@gillianflint_illustration

CHELSEA CLINTON is the author of the #1 *New York Times* bestseller *She Persisted: 13 American Women Who Changed the World*; *She Persisted Around the World: 13 Women Who Changed History*; *She Persisted in Sports: American Olympians Who Changed the Game*; *Don't Let Them Disappear: 12 Endangered Species Across the Globe*; *It's Your World: Get Informed, Get Inspired & Get Going!*; *Start Now!: You Can Make a Difference*; with Hillary Clinton, *Grandma's Gardens* and *Gutsy Women*; and, with Devi Sridhar, *Governing Global Health: Who Runs the World and Why?* She is also the Vice Chair of the Clinton Foundation, where she works on many initiatives, including those that help empower the next generation of leaders. She lives in New York City with her husband, Marc, their children and their dog, Soren.

You can follow Chelsea Clinton on Twitter
@ChelseaClinton
or on Facebook at
facebook.com/chelseaclinton

ALEXANDRA BOIGER has illustrated nearly twenty picture books, including the She Persisted books by Chelsea Clinton; the popular Tallulah series by Marilyn Singer; and the Max and Marla books, which she also wrote. Originally from Munich, Germany, she now lives outside of San Francisco, California, with her husband, Andrea, daughter, Vanessa, and two cats, Luiso and Winter.

You can visit Alexandra Boiger online at
alexandraboiger.com
or follow her on Instagram
@alexandra_boiger

Read about more inspiring women in the

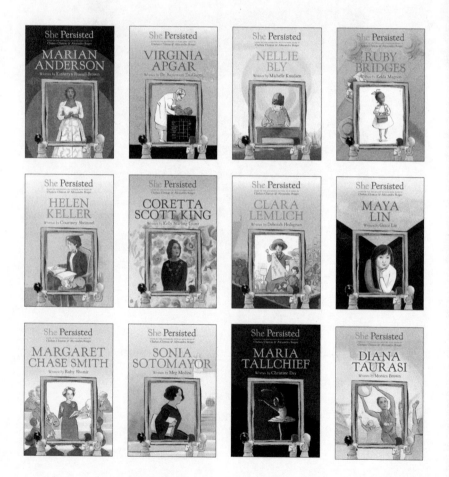

She Persisted series!

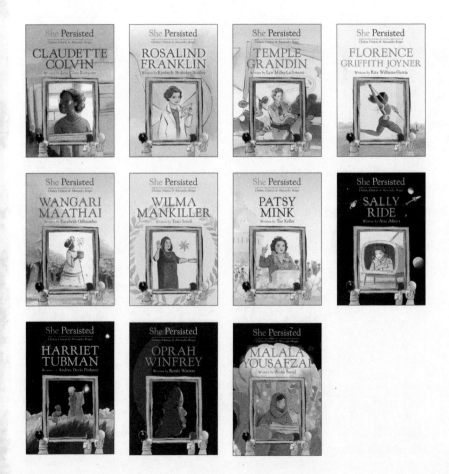